Fun to do

MASKS

Clare Beaton

CONTENTS

What You Will Need

Many of the masks in this book are made using the templates that you will find on pages 28-31, so do make sure that you have tracing paper. Also you will need a pencil, eraser and ruler for drawing and marking out, and a pair of compasses for measuring perfect circles. For cutting paper and thin card, you can use a pair of round-ended scissors, but you will need to ask a grown up to cut thick card for you with a craft knife. You will need glue or tape to fix things together, and paint and felt-tip pens for decorating the finished masks.

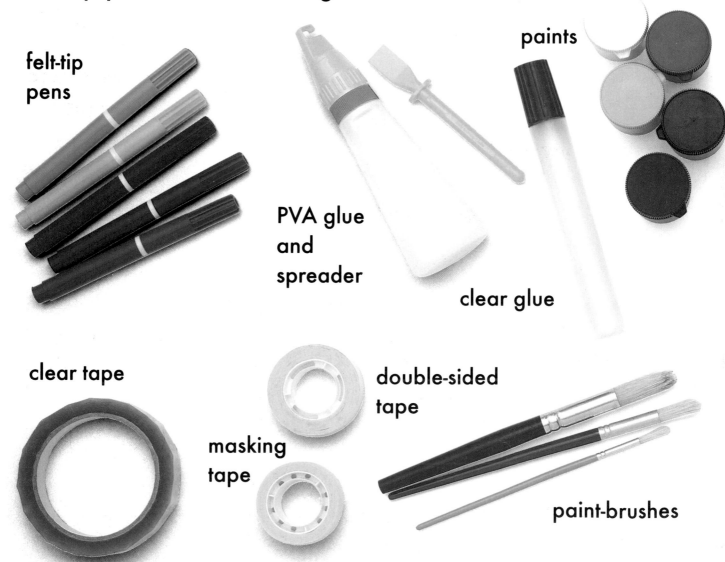

felt-tip pens

PVA glue and spreader

clear glue

paints

clear tape

masking tape

double-sided tape

paint-brushes

Other Useful Things

All sorts of things come in useful for making masks. Start a collection and keep adding to it. Store useful odds and ends in a box. Your collection might include:

Textured plastic packaging, colourful plastic bags, cardboard tubes, yoghurt cartons, bottle tops, jar lids, old newspapers and magazines, corrugated cardboard, gold and silver card, coloured card and paper, gummed paper, crêpe paper, tissue-paper, wool, string, cellophane and foil sweet wrappers, broken bead necklaces, tinsel, glitter, sticky shapes, buttons, sequins, felt, fabric scraps, pasta, raffia, garden sticks, pipe cleaners.

thick card

craft knife

metal ruler

pencil and eraser

scissors

bradawl

pair of compasses

tape measure

toothbrush

Remember

☆ Wear an apron and cover the work area.
☆ Collect together the items in the materials box at the beginning of each project.
☆ Always ask an adult for help when you see this sign [!]
☆ Clear up after yourself.

ruler

Bag Monster

To make *this giant mask* you'll need a large paper carrier bag with side and bottom gussets.

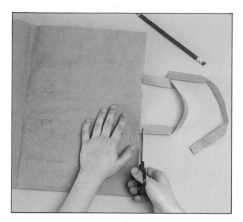

⚠️ **1** Put the bag over your head and ask an adult to draw on 2 small circles where your eyes are. Take the bag off and cut out the eye holes. Cut the handles off the bag.

2 Paint a frightening face on to the front of the bag. Leave to dry.

3 Cut 2 ears from the corrugated cardboard and decorate. Leave to dry.

4 Make a slit in the mouth. Cut a long tongue from red card, just wide enough to push through the monster's mouth.

5 Tape the ears to the side gussets of the bag.

6 Cut the coloured paper into strips of different lengths and widths. Curl by pulling firmly along closed scissor blades. Glue the curled paper all over the bag.

To give your friends a double fright paint a face on the back of the mask too.

5

Sunbeam

A golden mask to make you shine.

Materials

tinsel

corrugated cardboard

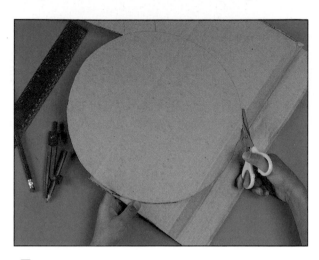

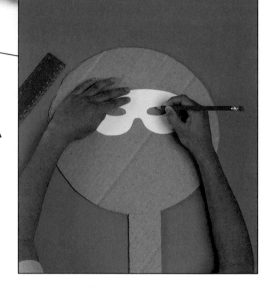

1 Draw a 28 cm-diameter circle on to the cardboard. Mark on a handle measuring 10 x 5 cm. Cut out.

2 Use template A on page 28 to trace off the position of the eyes on the circle about a third of the way down. Cut out.

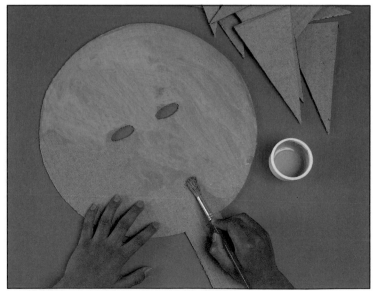

3 Cut triangles from cardboard. You will need enough to go all the way around the edge of the circle.

4 Paint the circle and the triangles yellow on one side. Leave to dry.

6

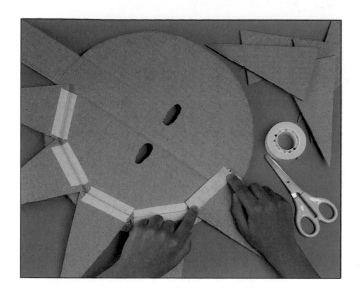

5 Tape the triangles to the unpainted side of the mask.

6 Paint a face on the front of the mask. Once the paint has dried glue tinsel around the face.

All that you need to make this stunning hand-held mask is corrugated cardboard and a bit of tinsel.

Mask on a Stick

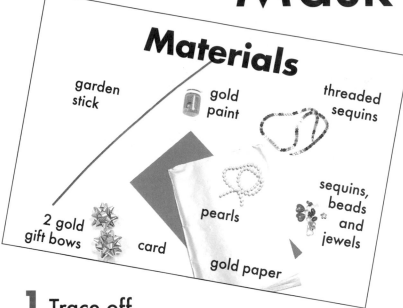

Materials

garden stick

gold paint

threaded sequins

2 gold gift bows

pearls

card

sequins, beads and jewels

gold paper

You can use all sorts of bits and pieces to decorate these simple-to-make eye masks.

1 Trace off template C on page 29 on to thick card to make a reuseable template. Draw around this template on to card and cut out. Stick the mask on to the gold paper and trim around the edges. Cut out the eye holes.

2 Decorate the front of the mask with the sequins, jewels, beads and pearls.

3 Stick a gold gift bow to each corner.

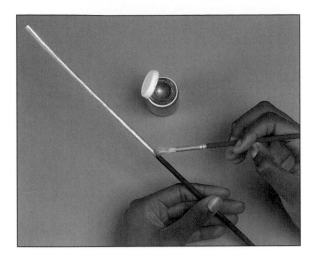

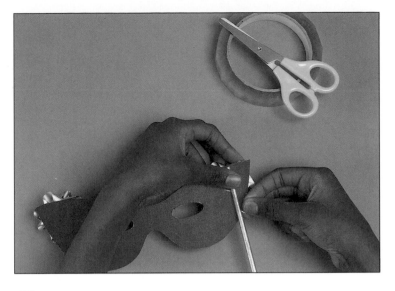

4 Cut the garden stick to about 30 cm long. Paint gold and leave to dry.

5 Tape the stick to one side on the back of the mask.

The finished mask! The other mask shown has been decorated with plastic flowers and a plastic beetle left over from a Christmas cracker. Butterflies have been cut from coloured paper and taped to plastic-covered wire.

An eye mask simply decorated with flashes of foil.

9

Reindeer

A fun mask to make for Christmas.

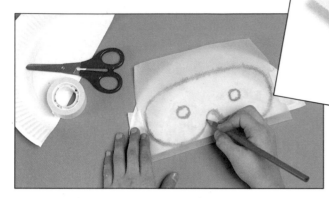

Materials

card

paper plate

thin elastic

1 Cut the plate in half. Tape a tracing of template B (page 28) to the rounded side of the plate. Draw around the eye holes and the bottom outline of the mask. Remove the tracing paper and cut out.

2 Paint the rounded side of the plate brown. Leave to dry.

3 Cut 2 ears from the card (template page 29). Paint brown and leave to dry, then paint the centre of the ears pink.

4 Trace off the antler template on page 29. Cut 2 from the card and paint both sides red. Leave to dry.

5 On the unpainted side of the mask, glue the antlers to the top and the ears to each side.

6 Make a small hole on either side of the mask. Tie a double knot at one end of a piece of elastic. From the front of the mask, thread the elastic through one hole to the other and secure with a double knot.

Spread a little Christmas cheer with this reindeer mask.

Christmas Tree Mask

Stick 2 card Christmas trees to the back of the mask. Decorate the trees with gold thread and small bead balls. Glue a paper frill or tinsel around the mask.

Materials

silver paper

silver stars

thin elastic

paper plate

thin black card

Batty

A super mask for Hallowe'en.

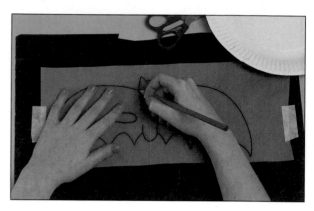

1 Trace off the bat template on page 29 on to the black card. Cut out.

2 Cut the plate in half and paint the rounded side dark blue. Leave to dry.

3 Make a hole on either side of the plate and thread through the elastic (see page 11, step 6).

4 Glue the bat on to the painted side of the plate so that the eye holes come just below the cut edge. Leave the wing tips unglued so that the bat looks as if it is flying.

5 Cut a crescent moon from silver paper.

6 Stick the moon and the silver stars on to the blue plate above the bat.

Adapt the look to become a living spider's web.

Bird-of-Paradise

Materials

coloured card

coloured paper

thin elastic

A fantastic mask that will make your budgie jealous!

1 Trace off template C on page 29 on to card and cut out.

! **2** Trace off the beak template on page 30 on to coloured paper and cut out. Ask an adult to score along the lines marked on the beak.

3 Fold the card along the scored lines to make the beak shape.

4 Cut long and short spikes from coloured paper. Glue these card 'feathers' to the top corners of the mask, overlapping them as you go.

14

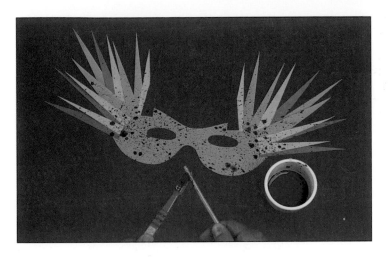

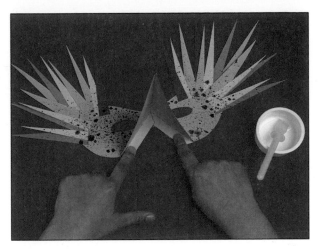

5 Dip a toothbrush into paint. Splatter the paint over the mask by gently pushing a paint-brush handle away from you along the head of the toothbrush. Leave to dry.

6 Put glue along the tabs on the beak and stick it to the centre of the mask between the eye holes. To fit the elastic, see page 11 (step 6).

Why not have a go at making other bird masks. For the toucan mask, use the beak template on page 30. Try fringing the edges of small pieces of paper to make the feathers.

Butterfly Wings

A beautiful butterfly mask that is sure to get you noticed.

Materials

2 pipe cleaners

sticky shapes

coloured paper

thin elastic

1 Trace off the template on page 28 on to a piece of folded coloured paper. Cut out. Open the paper to reveal the butterfly.

2 Tear strips and circles from coloured paper.

3 Stick the torn paper on to the front of the mask to decorate it. As you build up the pattern make sure that it is the same on both sides of the fold line.

4 Trim the ends of the paper strips to the shape of the butterfly wings.

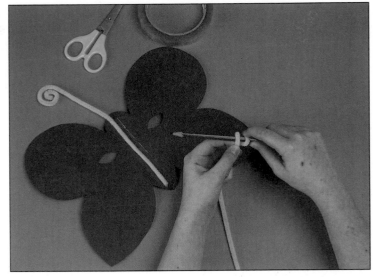

5 To finish decorating the mask add sticky shapes to it.

6 Curl one end of the pipe cleaners around a pencil. Tape the uncurled ends to the back of the butterfly.

To fit the elastic to the finished mask, follow the instructions on page 11 (step 6).

Fantastic Fox

A full face mask that will fox your friends! How long will it take them to guess who is beneath those whiskers?

1 Trace off the template on page 30 on to card and cut out. Carefully cut along the marked lines.

2 Overlap the card at each slit and tape together to make a shallow bowl shape.

3 Use the template on page 30 to cut 2 ears from card. Cut along the marked lines, overlap and tape together.

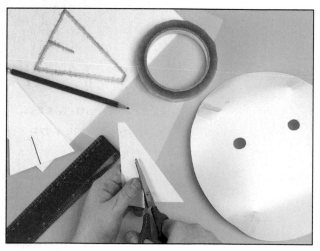

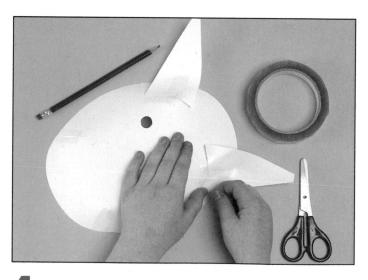

4 Tape the ears to the top of the front of the mask.

5 To make a nose, tape the cup on to the mask below the eye holes.

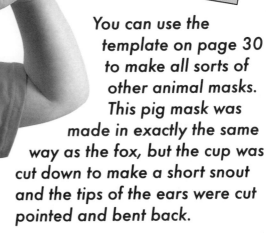

7 Make 3 small holes on either side of the cup nose with the point of a pencil. Cut the pipe cleaners in half and push through the holes for whiskers.

To fit the elastic to the finished mask, follow the instructions on page 11 (step 6).

6 Decorate the top half of the mask with brown paint. Leave to dry then paint the tip of the nose black.

You can use the template on page 30 to make all sorts of other animal masks. This pig mask was made in exactly the same way as the fox, but the cup was cut down to make a short snout and the tips of the ears were cut pointed and bent back.

19

Pasta Face

Dried pasta shapes arranged in a collage have been used to make this exciting tribal mask.

raffia

Materials

transparent plastic packaging

corrugated cardboard

thick paper

dried pasta shapes

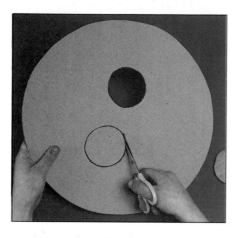

1 Cut a large circle 31 cm in diameter from the corrugated cardboard. Cut 2 large holes 3.5 cm apart in the centre of the circle.

2 Cut 2 squares from the plastic packaging to fit over the eye holes and tape on to the back of the mask.

3 Paint the front of the mask white and leave to dry. Now paint around the eye holes and add a big mouth.

4 Stick pasta shapes all over the mask to make a pattern. Use hollow pasta tubes around the eyes.

20

5 Cut the raffia into short lengths. Fold in half and push into the tube pasta.

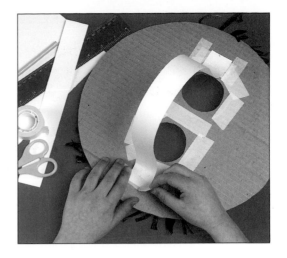

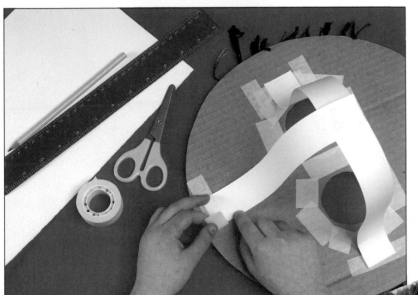

6 Tape a wide strip of paper about 50 cm long to either side of the eye holes on the back of the mask. Try on the mask to make sure it fits you. Adjust the paper strip if necessary.

7 Take a 30 cm-long paper strip and tape one end of it to the centre of the first strip, and the other end to the top edge of the mask.

This mask should come with a warning 'Guaranteed to make you jump!'

Bug Eyed

If you've ever wondered what a fly's world looks like, this is your chance to find out.

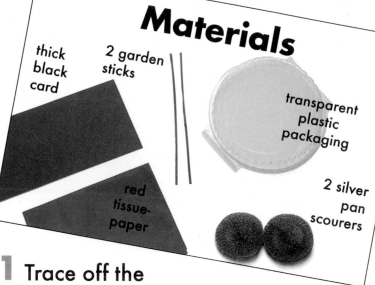

Materials

thick black card

2 garden sticks

transparent plastic packaging

red tissue-paper

2 silver pan scourers

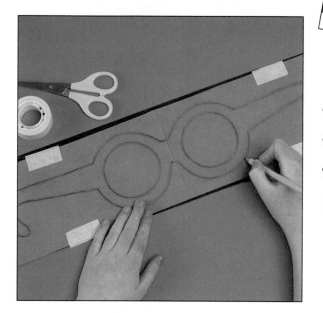

1 Trace off the template on page 31 on to a piece of folded tracing paper. Tape the tracing to the card and go over the outline. Remove the tracing and cut out.

[!] **2** To make hinged arms for the glasses, ask an adult to use a metal ruler and a craft knife to score a line on either side of the frames. Bend the card carefully along each scored line.

3 Glue the pan scourers to the front of the frames and press down firmly. Leave to dry.

4 Glue a garden stick between 2 strips of tissue-paper and leave to dry. Trim the edge of the paper close to the stick at the bottom, widening out towards the top. Cut into a curve at the top. Make 2.

5 Fringe the paper all the way around the edges. Tape the antennae to the back of the glasses.

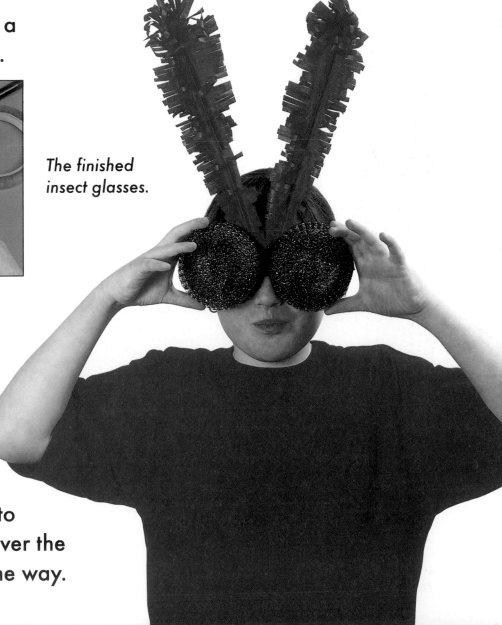

The finished insect glasses.

6 Lay a piece of transparent plastic over an eye hole and roughly mark on the shape. Cut out a circle of plastic slightly larger than the marked shape and tape to the back of the mask. Cover the other eye hole in the same way.

Happy and Sad

Materials

cardboard box

silver and gold shiny paper

thin elastic

How are you feeling today? This mask will keep everyone guessing.

⚠ **1** Trace off the template on page 31 on to folded tracing paper . Tape the tracing on to the box with the fold line laying on a corner edge. Go over the outline of the mask to mark it on to the box. Remove the tracing paper. Ask an adult to cut out the mask for you using a craft knife.

3 Paint a face on to the mask. Show a happy, upward-curving mouth on the red side and a sad, down-turned mouth on the blue side.

2 Paint one half of the mask red and leave to dry. Then paint the other half blue.

24

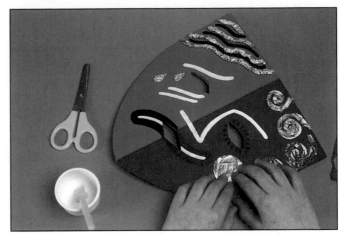

4 Twist together silver paper strips and glue to the blue side to make strands of wavy hair. Scrunch up 2 balls of silver paper to make teardrops and glue to the cheek.

5 Glue curls of twisted gold paper strips to the red side of the mask for hair. Cut a gold paper circle and glue to the cheek.

There are lots more 'contrast' masks that you could make. This one shows the night on one side and the day on the other. Why not make one of your own to show the difference between winter and summer?

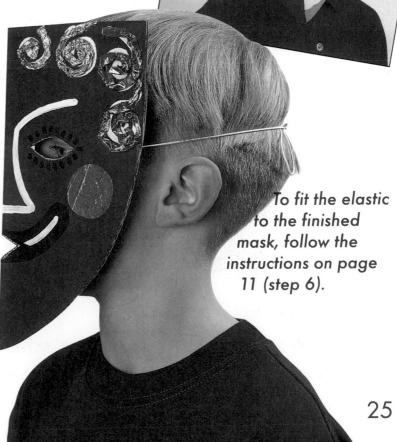

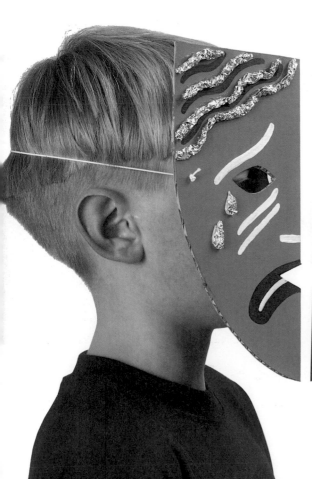

To fit the elastic to the finished mask, follow the instructions on page 11 (step 6).

Clown

One mask that is sure to make them laugh!

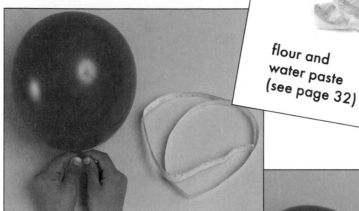

Materials

multi-coloured plastic bags

flour and water paste (see page 32)

newspaper

balloon

! **1** Measure around your head just above your ears. Blow up the balloon until it measures the same size as your head. Tie the end of the balloon in a knot.

2 Brush the balloon with paste and cover with small strips of newspaper. Add another 3 or 4 layers. Leave to dry out in a warm place for at least 24 hours.

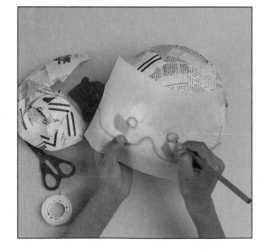

3 Cut off the bottom third of the balloon. Use template B on page 28 to trace off the eye holes and the bottom outline of the mask.

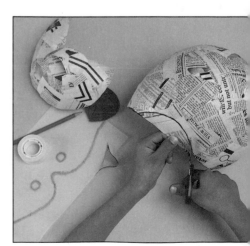

4 Continue the line around the sides of the balloon, curving up over your ears. Cut out.

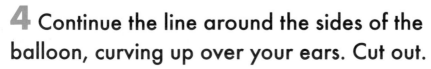

5 Paint the outside of the balloon white and leave to dry. Now mark on eyelashes and high curved eyebrows.

6 To make the hair, cut the plastic bags into long strips. Fold the strips in half, gather the folded ends together and glue along the inside edge of the mask.

TIP BOX
If you find that the papier mâché balloon is a snug fit, you can glue the hair to the outside edge instead.

Why not make a complete clown of yourself? Use face paints to cover the lower half of your face. Pin a ribbon bow tie to your T-shirt and wear a small party hat on top of the mask.

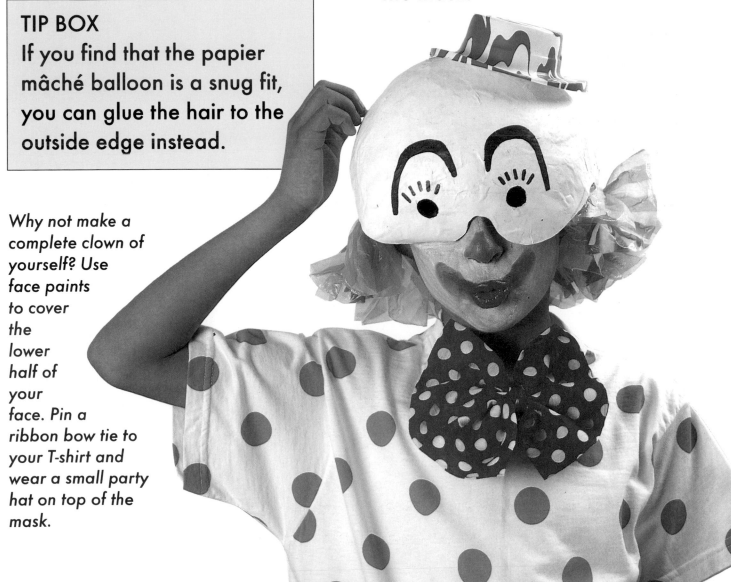

Templates

For instructions on how to trace a template turn to page 32.

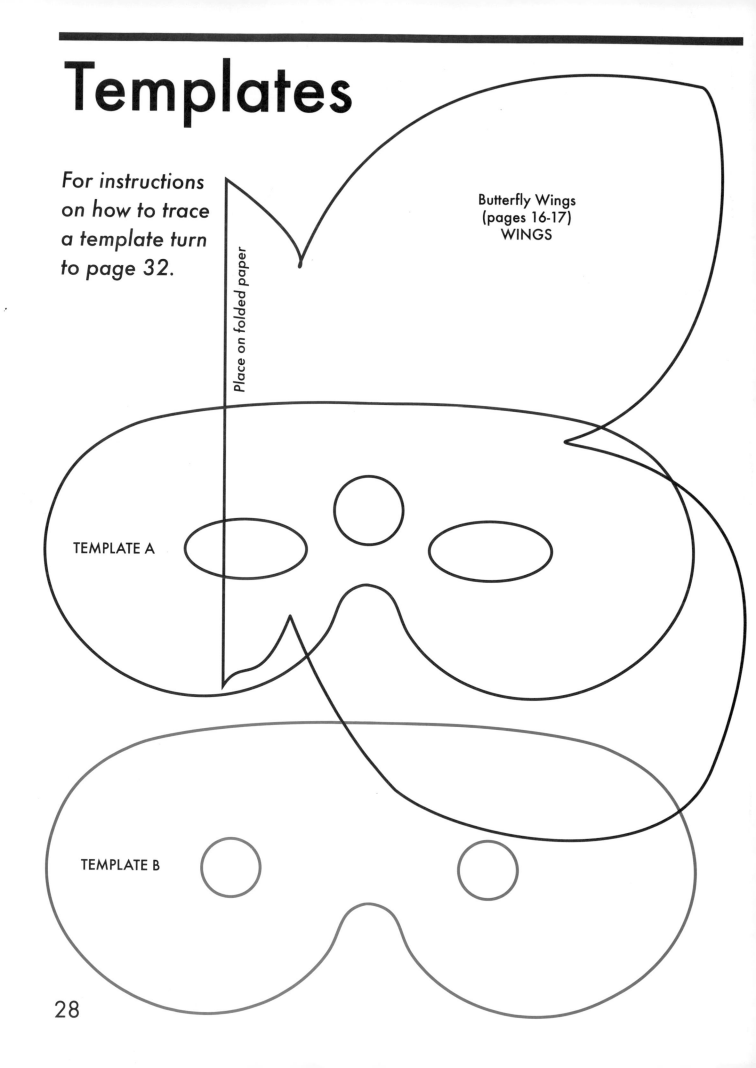

Place on folded paper

Butterfly Wings
(pages 16-17)
WINGS

TEMPLATE A

TEMPLATE B

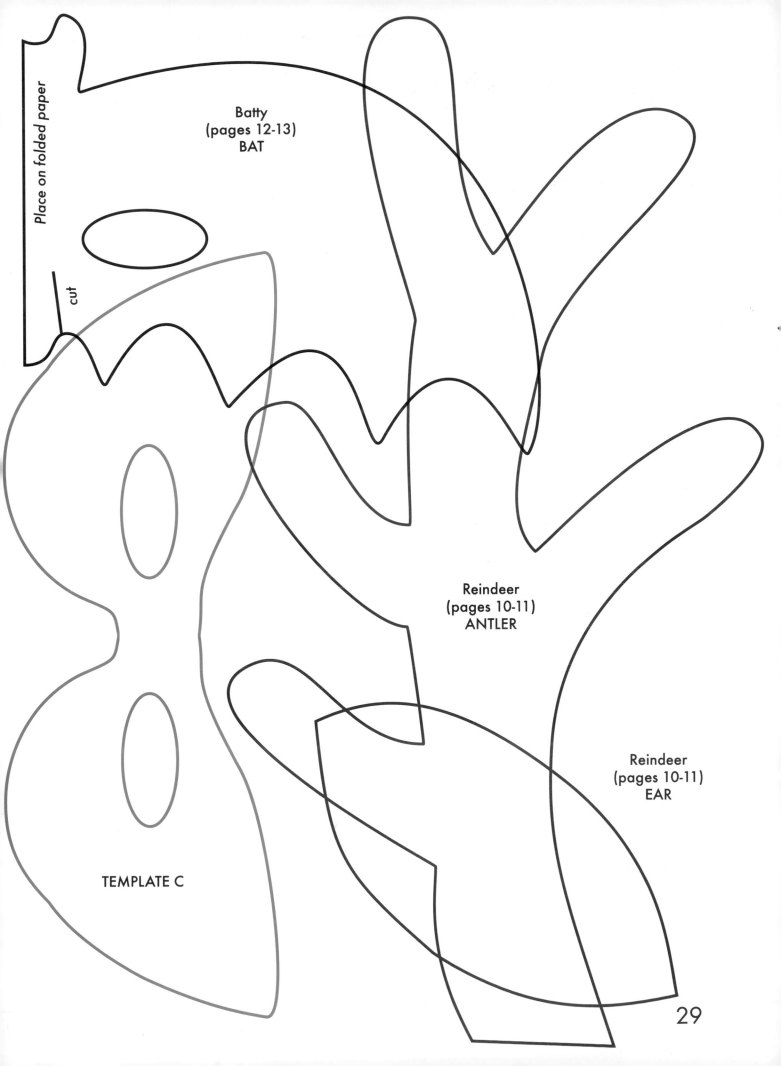

Place on folded paper

cut

Batty
(pages 12-13)
BAT

Reindeer
(pages 10-11)
ANTLER

Reindeer
(pages 10-11)
EAR

TEMPLATE C

29

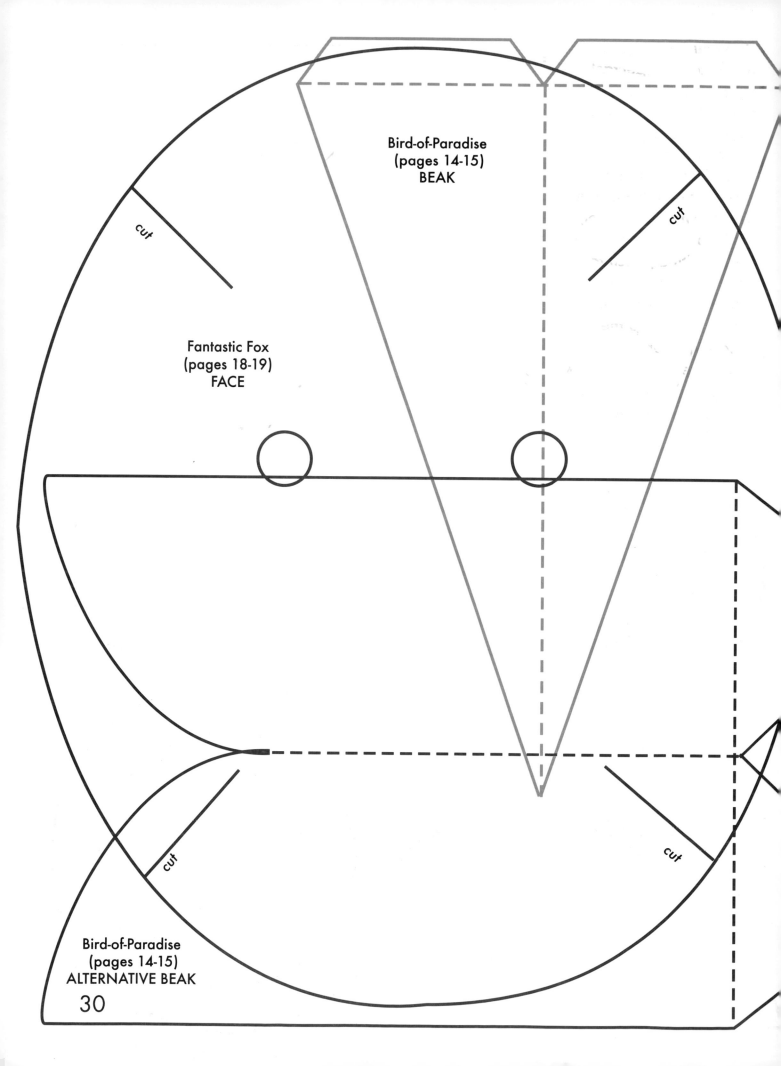

Bird-of-Paradise
(pages 14-15)
BEAK

cut

cut

Fantastic Fox
(pages 18-19)
FACE

cut

cut

Bird-of-Paradise
(pages 14-15)
ALTERNATIVE BEAK

30

To make a tracing of the face and spectacle templates on this page, fold a piece of tracing paper in half. Lay the folded edge on the dotted line and trace around the outline. Turn the tracing paper over, and go over the outline firmly with a pencil to transfer it on to the other half of the tracing paper. Open up the tracing paper. The completed outline is now ready to be transferred on to card or paper in the usual way.

Happy and Sad
(pages 24-25)
ONE SIDE OF FACE

Bug Eyed
(pages 22-23)
SPECTACLE FRAME

Fantastic Fox
(pages 18-19)
EAR

cut

Advice to Parents

Most of the masks in this book are made using the templates on pages 28 to 31. Many of the projects show how the template can be used in a slightly different way to create an often quite different mask. Do encourage your child to further adapt the templates to create masks unique to them.

The information on this page is designed to help you to encourage your child to get the most from mask-making.

Tools and Materials

Paint From a small selection of paints – red, yellow, blue, black and white – all other colours can be obtained by mixing. Encourage your child to explore colour mixing for herself. Poster paints are ideal for painting all the projects in this book. Always ensure that paint has dried before going on to the next step in the project.

Felt-tip pens A set of felt-tip pens is a good idea for adding fine features to masks. You can use felt-tip pens instead of paints to decorate all the masks in this book, especially if your child can't wait for paint to dry (a particularly good idea for the very young child).

Glue Solvent-free PVA adhesive is recommended as it is versatile, clean, strong and safe.

Scissors For the sake of safety children should use small scissors with round-ended metal blades and plastic handles. Although these are fine for cutting paper and thin card, they will not cut thick card and this is best done by you. This will often require a craft knife. Use a metal ruler to provide a straight cutting edge. If you do not have a cutting mat, use an old chopping board or very thick card to protect the work surface beneath. Regularly change the craft knife blade for a clean, sharp edge.

Paper and card Try to keep both white and coloured paper in the house. Do recycle paper whenever possible. Make use of off-cuts of wallpaper for example. Coloured card can be expensive: old cereal packets, folded flat, are perfect when thin to medium card is needed. Simply paint the unprinted side of the card whatever colour is required.

Papier Mâché

Papier mâché is made from old newspapers and a flour and water paste. To make this smooth, slightly runny paste you will need approximately 2 heaped tablespoons of plain white flour to 100 ml water. Gradually add the water to the flour and mix well. Do make sure that the papier mâché has dried out completely before decorating. This will take about 24 hours in a dry, warm place such as an airing cupboard.

Using a Pair of Compasses

A pair of compasses is a good tool for marking out a perfect circle. The diameter of a circle is the measurement taken across its centre. The pair of compasses needs to be fixed at half the measurement of the diameter. Keep the point firmly in contact with the paper and slowly move the pencil arm around to form the circle. Alternatively draw around a dinner plate to make a large circle, or a tea plate to make an average-sized circle, or a yoghurt pot for a small circle.

Making a Tracing

To make a tracing from the templates on pages 28-31 lay a piece of tracing paper over the required template. Draw around the outline with a pencil. Turn over the tracing paper and scribble over the pencil outline. Turn the tracing paper over once again and lay it down on to the paper or card that you want to transfer the tracing to. It is often a good idea to keep the tracing in place with masking tape. Carefully draw around the pencil outline. Remove the tracing paper. The outline of the traced shape on the card may be quite faint. Go over it with black felt-tip pen if necessary. It is often a good idea to make a reusable template. Transfer the tracing on to thick card. Cut out and label the card template and keep it in a safe place. Use the card template to draw around as often as it is needed.

Fastening a Mask

Elastic is the most convenient way to fasten the finished mask. The best type of elastic to use is hat elastic which is available from haberdashery stores. The way to fit the elastic has been described in detail in step 6 of the Reindeer mask on page 11. The best way to make holes in card is with a bradawl. Lay the card on a bed of modelling clay. This will prevent the work surface getting damaged. To strengthen the holes, cover with masking tape at the back of the mask. An alternative to elastic, card strips made into a type of headband, is given in Pasta Face (see page 21).

To my children:
Jack, Kate and Thomas

Reprinted 1996 by Merehurst Limited
Ferry House, 51-57 Lacy Road, Putney, London SW15 1PR

© Copyright 1994 Merehurst Limited
ISBN 1 898018 20 0

Project Editor: Cheryl Brown
Designer: Anita Ruddell
Photography by Jon Bouchier
Colour separation by P & W Graphics Pty Ltd, Singapore
Printed in Italy by G.Canale & C. SpA

The publisher would like to thank the staff and children of Riversdale Primary School, London Borough of Wandsworth, for their help in producing the photographs for this book.